# Two Generations from Slavery

## A book of poems

Dedication

This book is dedicated to the whole of my beloved family and the many gifts and talents the most high has bestowed upon us. From the chefs that have turned the simplest of meals into family gatherings, the educators who have passed down knowledge and history of our tree, to the seamstresses, tailors, artists, musicians, and poets. I thank you all for most importantly overstanding that the true values in life lie with family.

First and foremost I want to thank the most high for his creations. And for the journey of decision. May you be pleased with my work knowing you are my inner workings.

Second I want to acknowledge, thank and honor
my parents. If not for your travels I could never be. My father John Hodge those passed down paws. All your children have bruised knuckles.
My mother Barbara "Grannae" Morales who is truly everything a nurturer could be I thank you for my life, my siblings, and for all you have instilled in us.

Third I want to put a big squeeze on all my aunts and uncles for laying hands on my mold. You are all for your own reasons, honorable to me. Special shout out to my poetic influence Chester "Chess" Smalls. Thank you for being the true meaning of encouragement.

To my siblings, my lifeline, my five brothers and two sisters, I apologize for the chocolate icing (inside joke).
Dahoo "JstJah" Smalls you have always been my right hand. Thank you for always holding me down. Gb forever.
Ngina "Geesus" Morales, you have taught me so much the most high could not have gifted me a better big sis.
Raheem "Danali" Morales you are my other side as if I was blessed with two rights. Take your time and recognize your genius.
Ayesha "Big Eash" Morales you have always been like a big little sister and I love you for that.
Benjamin "Beny Bermuda" Morales, the dopest mc on the crustal plates. You have always been ahead of your time.
Jabril "Jay Bang" Morales you remind me of myself in a lot of ways. Family man and protector. I am proud of the man you have grown into.
Fard "SoTrue" Morales your fashion is clearly unmatched. Which is pretty unique for a style like someone who has been here before.
I am blessed to say the least we are genetically connected.

My 2 sons,
Kaleek "Deuce" Morales and Samir "Niem" Morales, you are my legacy. May you both be greater than your father.

Last but not least,
I'd like to send a special shout out to my extended family in the poetry and arts community. Too many to list without missing anyone but I want you all to know you inspire me to be great.

Two generations From Slavery is a literary journey unlike any other that you have ever experienced. Twelve of the Twenty One poems in this book have partner Haiku in the simultaneously released book Wittie Haiku. The poems with corresponding haiku have stars beside them on the title page and the haiku number at the bottom of the actual page. Ideally, you will read the poem and then go to the haiku book to read the matching haiku. I hope you enjoy this added bit of interaction.

Table of Contents

0. A Piece of Mind

1. Respect

2. The Outfit and the Instilled *

3. Dropping the Ball

4. Mindfood (Food For Thought) Pt. 1

5. Media

6. Race *

7. Momentum *

8. Knuckle Up (Fists to the Sky)

9. Bio: Degradable

10. Head of a King *

11. Drapetomania

12. Fit for Vocabulary

13. Mirrors and Windows

14. Five Dollar Indian *

15. Manipulated entertainment *

16. Game or Gamers *

17. Provision *

18. Pray Me a Slave *

19. Mindfood (Food For Thought) Pt. 2

20. Nameless Bullets *

21. Chemtrails *

## *0. A Piece of Mind*

400 years of physical slavery,
a history of downgrading.
Enforced police brutality and programmed education.
To seating us on the bus.
Our living quarters were rotten.
Took us from the lands we homed,
to slave and pick your cotton.
Rapists of our queens.
Killers of our children.
Starved and whipped our ancestors.
Yet we're the strongest living.
For we've took the worst,
the longest time.
Who else could have lasted.
Jailing our fathers and sons,
or laying them in caskets.
Leaving our women to lean on you for money and food.
Corrupted us with your drugs.
You thought you had us fooled.
Two wrongs don't make a right and we seat far from fair.
You are grafted from us.
We are original here.
Lied to blind us in the light,
while you worked in the dark.
Sponged us for entertainment.
You've branched from our bark.
We're not all careless though,
some need concentration.
Fearing the New World when they know not what they're facing.
We need understanding.
For that we need listen.
We must pull together.
Trust and loyalty is missing.
We are bigger than this.
Civilization's mother and father.
There is no goal we can't achieve.
We just need to work harder.
For the only thing stopping us,
is us separated.
Lust, envy, greed, jealousy, hatred.
Their shadows are our laws.

For to know wrong one must have been wrong.
To purify oneself, won't determine if you’ll live long.
Yet it betters your chances.
For these streets are rough.
An empty head’s like a starved stomach and we've hungered long enough.
Feed your mind mental food, actual facts and history.
To live off opinion is to live in mystery.
Find out who you be and you’ll no longer be blind.
Once you have conquered this, freedom of the mind.

## *1. Respect*

Now I understand why growing up respect meant so much
When I look at youth and see how far from touch we've landed
But I don't blame them, I blame us
who got lost chasing notes marked In God We Trust
Entrusted in its power and people influence
which would aid and abet in said ruins
Generations in will be payment cashed in
Today's young men are like the ass in lion's skin
In relay we race with man's baton leverage
By time it got to them, they received the wrong message
Hunger set in and so prey was foreseen
And misinterpreted, the term by any means
Became dog-eat-dog,
wolves eat sheep
Some submissively embraced their meek
All young or innocent when lost to the street
We are so stretched out we'll need a million arm reach
To embrace the issue because the racing's the crime
Hustling through life but if era be mine
Please forgive me for smoking away our quality time
Those days it seems you came after the grind
Those nights I could have hugged you instead I chose a toilet
This could never make up, it's just a step forward
If our own ignorance prolonged this great nation
It's the choices we made for self-preservation
So for us to excel we have to address the problem
What's an American dream when reality got them
Growing statistics
drug and street violence victims
misled from school to the prison system
It's time for us to step up get out and get with them
And they will listen when you take the time to sit with them
So I'm gonna leave this insight for the overlook
When you walk with respect, it's hand and foot

## *2. The outfit and the instilled*

They say “one bad apple spoils the bunch”
But that didn't stop them from making your juice with it
Adding all these chemicals into a mix
of disguise nutrients to fool you with it
Effectively we are what we eat and the reactant feelings it induces
Yet you'll find more lemons squeezed in cleaning supplies
than you do in *said to be* lemon juices
See the blindfold is as masking as the packaging
Sleepwalkers land where ignorance lay comfy
This portion of the globe where more products are sold
That are illegal to consume in other countries
So who judge we, when lawyers lunch with your honor
Am I the only one who can see more than a case at stake
The scandals lined panels and under the table currency
In exchange for situations, set to assassinate
The thought process which has become as processed as the food
Obviously succumbed to a national menticide
We the decimated character bought stock in propaganda
And are now the purchasers of our own genocide
No more than the blind can see their own hands,
can deaf hear.
The dumb down came through pacification
Money, sex, drugs became the focal point thugs
Who unwarranted youth with aspiration
America remits yet she owes a deficit
So we must look to whom she pays out
For this rock of a continent was conquered and cultivated
To bring an abstracting chaos throughout

*56

## *3. Dropping the ball*

Okay so x-rays can scan down to the bone
Tell me why prison guards are still looking in inmate's asses
Almost everything you need or want to learn is online
Still we seek status in untaught classes
We're ready for war when it comes to our own
Yet it's our own we continue to put in caskets
Youth Development is not developing here
Impaired sight can see that without their glasses
From vote to post about our president's blackness
While Constitution has written us in as equal
We will chase that image til it is destroyed
I've learned misleading can control people
Now we fault the youth as if the blame isn't our own
Even cast shadows will bear reflection
Yet that injustice is fought to a moot point
Cause we are easily blinded with misdirection
We social media prey, lay in assembly
Astray from our revolutionary lives
Music and video tranced when we need to wake up
For all the uprise our ancestors fought for dies
We, the kept Negus of untaught lessons
Repeat history because our minds are enchained
Without combinations to free oneself
People who don't grow will talk of how you have changed
Too good to eat the same meal for two days
These days we don't even know survival
In fact we don't even know the meaning of faith
Until the moments in which life tries you
For we, like tree leaves, fell victim to gravity
Pulls of fantasies, lusts and vanities
Unsewn wounds exposed in sanities
Due to the roots grown from planted seeds
But we won't abandon the media
We like the way people think for us, it's fashioned to style you
If consequences don't exceed the fly of the feces attracted then what's the value
It's all image and appealing to the eye
How we have obviously ignored the message
Until we grab control of which way we are headed
Our babies will continue to be intercepted

## *4. Mindfood (Food For Thought) Pt. 1*

Eyes are looking but who's really seeking
Seems like you're seeing or are you just peeking
The road is narrow each side's wide as space
Speed and you'll stumble
patience is grace
Knowledge is food that the stomach can't settle
Brave master themselves while the scared waste their vessels
Our time may seem short though we are here for a purpose
Molded from clay dirt to now roam the surface
Life's subliminal read through man's creation
For screen concentration can be mind erasing
We are reflections arm, leg, leg, arm, head
Not just in ones complexion get underneath shed
Forfeit indulgence of a blind man's dream
Nor wonder in the wilderness of plots and schemes
More than a handful have tried to mentally escape
Eventually lids blink revealing same place same shapes
Not much has changed whether the mouth open or closed
You get saliva on your clothes or bacteria in lip folds
Roots of all evil pain the wrists of the tight fists
I mind you not to enter situations without exits
Pledges to Almighty for Allegiance have never been Ally
Instead it's as if a vast spread of global fungi
Has chained our mentality along with limited equality
Is slavery dead along with prejudice and mockery
Please taste this before a controlled substance
You will find the high to be more alluring with humbleness
I am the sun which keeps all planets aligned
My freedom, free-dome diluted divine

## *5. Media*

Smoke weed, get high, sip liqs, pass time
Media emphasizes enticed perversions
Politics, war crimes, the news plants fear in minds
Gangs commit genocide it's all coercion

Remove the blindfold, worldwide manipulation
Glamour, glitz, gold exposed exaggerations
Till you realize from those misinterpretations
What's real in life; it's your imagination
New jail cells for domes in captivation
Family values lost through generations
Social standing developed a segregation
Dishing out six degrees of separation
Babylon rose from slave to immigration
Best exterminations established infestations
Shackles slid off the mind in elevation
Media distracting the blind with taxation
New disease out got them lined like cabs waiting
No school for youth 'less you get them the vaccination
Countries been invaded through terrorist motivation
Falsified freedom embellished an imitation

Television known to be visual intoxication
Blatant foul language subliminal fornication
False Jews running everything Brothers in hibernation
Africa's children still dying of starvation
Most of black history's missing from education
Background checks for employment, discrimination
Government commits its own insubordination
Then they drew us in with Obama's inauguration
Same-sex marriage approved through legislation
Chemtrails dropping down poison precipitation
Skulls and crossbones are death implications
All over the clothes as if they trying to make a statement
Stars are misguiding our youth through entertainment
Pretend Heroes when our children need saving
Adult messages used in animation
Babies having babies let's deal with the situation

Police the globe tactics in effect think they're playing
Sacrificing Nations out for world domination
Earth ain't dying stop buying her expiration
Doomsday psychology keep us in enslavement
Patriot games arming rebels for liberation
Government scandals and covert operations
HAARP at work killing masses with radiation
Earthquakes, hurricanes, weather alterations
Practice makes perfect experiment is preparation
Cure is not an option the money's in medication
Hustle mentality is a pivotal obligation
Puppet strung to the oppressor's abomination

Smoke weed, get high, sip liqs, pass time
Media emphasizes, enticed perversions
Politics war crimes, the news plants fear in minds
Gangs commit genocide, it's all coercion

## *6. Race*

So now we view human
Race as a contest
From the sound of the gunshot
Aimed at the black man

Race me
Because you can not
Erase Me.
Trap me within labels
Defame me crazy.
Angry aggressive
Elusive, maniac.
Whatever's lessening.
For melanin
Must have set eyes
On your deception.
Nothing less of rescue
From human trafficking
Can deserve your 52 shots
Threw a front windshield.
You're choking the life
From my fear resisting body
While in custody of
Your ink blotted legal system.
Seems your Authority
Compromises my
Human equality.
Like cattle my existence
Has become your means
Of survival.
Bullwhipped into believing
I am bettered by your badge.
You've lost sight of the task
Trying to defend the shield.
Or was that an overseen mission
To be so polished up
It's shine blinds you.
To a white Hood
To terminate a black hoodie.
To a black hood
To try out your

White Hood instinct.
Hoodlum
To shoot the back out
A fleeing suspect.
Guilty til proven innocent
Never the other way
Around.
Reminders of captivity
Dealt by
Cruelties finest.
Then I remember
America
Main attracted slaves
So the pirate
Didn't have to
Catch them.
But that blanket wasn't
Half the size
To cover its truth.
Freedom hunger
Grew of eyes
In search of
Cultureless settings.
That savage in you
Thirsting defecation.
Or was it your very own
Blood in your saliva.
That drew the bath
Behind your Hellfire
And redrum sippings.
Have you not
Wasted enough life yet.
Have you not
Erased enough time yet.
You truly glutton it all.
Fattening your belly
With the marrow of the poor.
Thank God for the soul.
For which you truly
Can not own.
Even when you
Are pawnshop to
Proclaimed stardom.

There is no pay out
Beyond puppetry.
Nothing to hold onto
When God takes back.

So now we view human
Race as a contest.
From the sound of the gunshot
Aimed at the black man.

*59

## *7. Momentum*

The quantity of motion of a moving body
Measured as a product of mass and velocity
Today's fashion yesterday's atrocity
Forward motion with the weight of the world on top we
Speak of motivation without momentum in play
Seems quick as we've progressed we fell back to their way
For example in less than 365 days
Went from Django Unchained to 12 Years a Slave
So what fuels our engine cause you see the gas rates
It's a tightrope race between murder and rape
Further we skate from the path closer we see how we got here
Look at the dress code underwear became outerwear
So we sacrifice sacredness of what lies beneath
Though naked is the ocean you have to go deep for the reef
Some say sleep is death's cousin but can't see past their eyelashes
When you don't rest the body, the body crashes
As time pursues some hold onto their youth til the end
Meanwhile some youth will never be men
On a mission through prison
In coffins they're found
Domino effect ain't even realize the knock down
Profound minds in time find the exit to the maze
Which is usually an entrance into another maze
Hell's a notorious story well written on the page
In the blaze of glory there'll be no glory in the blaze
It's a sinful mule and lust riding at the reins
In search of the weak link they're just tugging on the chains
Willie Lynch influences smothering the brain
What some do to get a fix, some will do for fame
Substance abuse as a crutch could end up as a cane
Cause today peer pressure is like trying to dodge rain
It's all fun and games til you lose and you recap the plays
Probably pulled for a jay when you had the lay
Decisions affect the outcome still we stand divided
Ain't even room for discussion we've already decided
That simple minded attitude that I can do it myself
That got you comfortable as somebody else's help
Was wise but blind eyes can never see their condition
Like prayer without motion to take what god positioned for you
But human race sounds like a contest don't it
Not only do we condone competition we own it

So who's pushing the buttons yet selecting contestants
Every obstacle is a challenge to be taken with relevance
Like every life lived is a lesson for the lives behind it
We get protective of our future then we get reminded
They're plotting population control in democracy
I mean to build a casket to bear more than one body
Evil intentions are amongst us weapons armed and ready
Some usually don't pay attention till it affects directly
Broke the levees moved the surviving hell they displaced families
Cleaned up in time to party sounds like stolen land to me
He who stake claim and set forts in every land he roam
And it don't matter if you were born here this is not your home
This is Babylon where eyes are on the tainted prize
So migration to this cesspool should be no surprise
If everything's about a hustle then we're built to lie
Cause hustle means to manipulate for gain or rise
Words have meanings though we manipulate what they define
If you ain't teaching then you're thieving from the youthful mind
Be mindful of the message that you program in them
When motivating uphill you can kill momentum

*10

## *8. Knuckle Up (Fists to the Sky)*

The walls hollow with echo when spoken to
Even my laugh out loud voice is mute
My hugs non-existent, my humanity is challenged
Memes and emojis render me artificially intelligent
My original thoughts have become drive to ride along
Bearing fictitious tags for the brag and add-on
My hashtag winning while black lives lost grows
Drunk in false claimed triumph that honor role
Those life situations we live to die for
As if the grave is the rush man now lives for
Dead bones fully exposed like an eroded shore
Free in thought, sought early death in the eyes of the law
Dream in planted success stories, to deceiving the clone
Versus reality in vision when we step out our homes
Crabs in a barrel affected the ass climbed upon asses
Young become what they eat, while what's foul feeding masses
Ignorance drowns me to a norm, it's negligent
To conceive and accept my own self prejudice
Got me locked up so tight I'm mentally remanded
Subconsciously it's as if I'm in fear of a Black Planet
I forgot about the prints in sand my feet left
Barely caught that last breath as I bled to death
Choked up, I'm noose tucked under the chin today
Became organs to donate, cattle, prey
These were once strong hands when my voice was loud
I let my fist to the sky indicate my proud
With a lean so hard it could break my habits
Dome free in a land cultivated for captives
I could see in the sea of faces lost promise
So ahead of themselves they forgot to pay homage
From padlock minded to brainwashed and polished
Living that in fact which was said to be abolished
Those roots that stem is what law branches off
Ignoring the past is a blind move forth
So let's go back for land and not to loot
Back to planting seeds to harvest fruits
Teaching our youth to be true pursuers
Where human values outweigh computers

The programming starts with the at home message
Time spent tops any money invested
Love is what it takes for us to survive
Bring back that thrive knuckle up fist to the sky

## *9. Bio: Degradable*

Bio being biology
Being of study
From our melanated skin cells
To the smallest structural unit
Found centered in the body
Bio being biography
Meaning our story
From the beginning of our captivity
To the chains that bind us
To their claim today
Chained to degrade
Bio degradeable
Being of disrespect
We are disrespected beings
Pacified by the glare of the cake icing
That sight of pie slicing
that keeps us in contempt
THAT'S what his-story
Has accounted us for
Writ us in
Three fifths
In a Fifth Third Banking Society
And mocked us with a black card
For the blind pocket spending
Reminders of a selfless King
Who gifted body's weight in gold
Shameful to think today
That here
Here we are
Found a living
biodegradable people
Capable of being decomposed
We've become the living organisms
decomposing each other
The, instrumenting for
Feeding drugs to one another
Decomposing the genius
That God has created
Unlearneth of the lessons

set forth by our belated
We are decomposing
By bacteria in the products we use
Air and water chemicals
And in the foods we eat
Decomposed in our own dreams
Habits and their influence
Their doctrines
It's no wonder we can't get no sleep
Decomposed in year round Christmas
Lighting atop patrol vehicles
That false sense independence
Every time we see them
Decomposed in the numerous
Scandalous officials
Crazy strawing the law
Unless it's us who need them
Decomposed in choosing roles
That belittle the black image
And influence in our behavior
And the way we think
Decomposed by the lack
of education of self
That has us selling ourselves
Back to the chain link
Decomposed in the illness of contesting each other
Clouded spots defecting vision
It's a nebula structure
Decomposing our accomplishments
And ancestral ways
So what will be of your bio set forth in your obituary
I pray you lack degrade

*93

## *10. Head of a king*

Heavy weighs the crown on the head of a king
Yet and still he raises his head to speak to his people
He addresses them not of what it is he has achieved
But what it took to reach his achievement
His kingdom not of inheritance
For to hand down what he bore
Would be hard to conceive as Royal
The world is cruel
And minuscule of man can appear
When the earth is ripping the sneakers off you
His life is a battlefield his chest his heart's shield
Armor pierced from swords clashed
It'd be eves for a night's still
Poise as stones like spat arrows are tossed
As if protected by force field
They bounce off his hardened vessel
He had been stoned before
And just as those wounds
They will soon scab and heal
Till they're but scars on the mental
Heavy weighs the crown on the head of a king
Yet and still he raises his head to speak to his people
He addresses them not to chain them to his fate
But to remind them their roots
Are down rooted to passage
Unsheltered from the storm
Many a storm have been weathered
Chariot riders blind quested
Glanced laughed and rode passed it
Placid is the man in tune with life's rhythm
Though his unorthodox beat
Was a misunderstood harmony
Set free in his dome wasn't free in his home
So he gave all who billed
A send-off with no obsequey
Obviously freedom was a dumb, deaf, blind fold
To slave mentality and web man's eyes closed
The messenger was owl and it valued a lie sold
Bought by Average Joe chained to pocket the land stole
Sweat off the brow

Heavy weighs the crown on the head of a king
Yet and still he raises his head to speak to his people
He addresses them not of pity for condition
But to recondition the pitiful state
In which they've fallen
Seems the misled horse drank a pool of manipulation
Intoxicating the thoughts of that
In which it heard calling
Morning come at Daybreak and laminations of Lost Ones
When observantly Lost Ones
Today is not an illusion
While the media coerces
What's sexy, cool and appropriate
Unfortunately the youth get
Caught up in the confusion
Often man can appear to be other than man
Women other than women
No sense of indigenous
Character stature purpose mishandled
Prime example when cattlemen
Leave their herd to wander off in the wilderness
Sheep amongst the wolves
Fall to snakes in high grass but then
Fear, greed, religion
Weaved a quilt of divided men
The American dream
Was a nightmare disguised gem
Obvious we still three fifths
In the eyes of them
Heavy weighs the crown on the head of a king
Yet and still he raises his head to speak to his people
He addresses them not with the burden of truth
Though he spoke the truth so their burdens may be lifted
It's big business for men who sit in cahoots
Though at odds same objective
"Keep the mental imprisoned"
Laws are shadows of the wicked
Tax is tariff, new description
New narcotic, new prescription
But y'all still don't get it
See we fighting over complexion
Permeated misdirection
In attempt to stall the mind

And bring demise to the gifted
For you are the gifted
Mouth of a King, ears of the people
Yet in appearance King
Wasn't who spoke before the people
Those who bypass presentation
Find the substance lane
The most intricate of subjects
Hide in covers, plain
He wasn't dressed of the clergy
Attire opposing clean
Though his thoughts and words
Were more than reverent
He was genuine in speech
Emphasized aggressively
Those who live by the day
Kill their future in the present
In this accelerated world
Few would have stopped
To get the lesson
Looking upon this King
One would mistake for a peasant
Yet never since school
Was it cool to be ingenious
Or was it truly genius
Who be keeper of cool
See when you dream their dream
You build their corporation
Their dream that's when they
Truly have taken you for the fool
The slew began with alcohol
Moving forth to smokers cough
Injections in arms
Up the nose their mind's gone
This abuse of cloudy vision
Induced however form
Switching natural consciousness out the norm
Helped to push forth the pawn
He said our mind's in a sling
Heavy weighs the crown on the head of a king

*13

## *11. Drapetomania*

Samuel A. Cartwright diagnosed it Drapetomania
Said fleeing captivity was a negro mental illness
Which obviously explains my sick to the stomach
Regurgitation found in this spillage
His 1851 theoretical bullshit which could only have come from a demon's equal
Prescribed the audacity of a documented cure for
So called whipping the devil out my people
Where amputated big toes were justifiable hindrance to those who tried to leave
Stating slaves should be submissive, fearing God in their masters
And if not then made to be
Some seedless trick knowledge to maintain oppression and persuade in its cruelty more likely
Adrenaline pumping the cold vein inhumane acts picnic engraved for the viewing psyche
Cartwright's pseudo-scientific, racial theory writ to master lock on black minds
Which was then found in agreement amongst his peers a many years before it's demise
Demon-strating the mind today's politician stem from that stacked deck we know what the deal is
Eroding the planet from atmosphere to core in true definition of what ill is
Yet he blamed it sickness of the mind to take flight with unwanted punishment on you
Behold the presence of unadulterated hatred imposed by that illegitimate uncle
Ole Sam, face in disgust, finger-pointing your direction
In Top Hat, a symbol of Illusion and deception
White striped to represent cotton white supremacy
Bloodlines of Indian and African ancestry
Lay behind the stars badging those overseers
Square in a rectangle of contrast believers
Who say it's maniac thinking to flee this treatment
Kidnap, rape, game, labor and beatings
It's clear you're aware and cease to see that plight
Back when running for your life was the start of the fight

## *12. Fit for vocabulary*

About time we wake up out this dream and set focus on bettering
Black community instead of moving and settling
Exiting a place does not mean you escape
Especially when people you know fall victim to the bait
Evaluate Laws of Attraction because image isn't everything
Let's be mindful of the direction in which we are pedaling
For what we instill young will become adolescent
Tangled in the weaves of early deception
Talking animals on TV playing on kids intellect
May seem harmless til you have to go and correct
Programmed birds-and-bees in terms of sex
Storks dropping off babies no telling what's next
Worker ants moving their dollar in every aspect
All reference to lesser life forms we mimicked the insects
And they swat us down when our smarts challenge their ego
Then bloodsuck us for everything, leeches, gnats, mosquitoes
Kill and conquering the untaught, predatory evil
Pinned backs against the wall and that's why people
Been climbing on one another segregated in turmoil
Don't want to help better you they want to be better you for you
What's become of humanity, comparison and replacement
We are so judgemental of God's creations
Fear and ignorance reciprocate our contemplation
And we don't stand up for sit-down conversations
Yet we jump on one another over words once spoken
Pride will kill you like a brain aneurysm growing
While the focus lies on fashion, stones, cars and phones
Bills packed in the mailbox back us in our own home
Chained to everything that entraps us on this slave ship
Lead by the word "can't"
that man felt was fit for vocabulary

## *13. Mirrors and windows*

People will set sight upon you like sun over ocean face
And judge the beauty of you like jurors of an open case
Sentence you to hell as if they've visited the place
Then weigh your life expectancy like a plant in a vase
Captured by the lens, nothing can appear any clearer
Than observing the situation in the motion, picture
How snapshots scan the brain then thoughts trigger
Easier to stare through someone's window than to look in the mirror
Ain't a vision given to man can peek into the soul
Your own eyes can deceive you when you play that role
Unfair is judgement, if you pay that toll
Fact is that is usually another opinion, sold
To propaganda consumers of the world today
Faith, politics, scandals, what the famous say
Where you been, bought, ate, even whose birthday
Who had a baby, got arrested, or was killed today
Yesterday's message was delivered only misdirected
Naked images in windows often distract intelligence
And become the mirror effect of the less intelligent
In search of a reference to find their relevance
We're fed the cover story, see footage, read the comments then
Bandwagon someone's death for likes and acknowledgements
Kidnappings, domestic violence, more murders than natural deaths
Ain't hard to be today with what mainstream
projects
Mirrors reflect lighting and movement, imagery reflects in the mind
Scales and balances got us out killing our own kind
Indoctrinated thoughts like sight when you're blind
Overseers been hunting down slaves a long time
Nowadays find there's no blinds on that window
Apparently it's normal as the clouds and winds blow
Manipulated shadows of wrongs come to pass
These shattered mirrors path of broken glass
And we bare footprint through the sands of souls
This is the difference in mirrors and windows

## *14. Five Dollar Indian*

A-cross the Atlantic with specific purpose
They land afar and on a land foreign to their widened irises
Natives they welcome though no well comes
Just plague as they play on their ill-begotten kindness
In time this voyage will be marked historic
Columbus minus the Moorish navigated influence
It was Nina, Pinta, Santa Maria
Set a sail under European issuance
A distance no man from their inhabitants
Had yet to experience nonetheless life was clearly there
Out of the cold of Spain this Italian/Spaniard claimed
He'd discovered a Western hemisphere
They docked where there was no docks
Or ports just the indigenous people of the region
Who waved on as the waves clashed their boats
Unaware of the tyranny they'll sit amongst by evening
Exchanging medicines and crops for blanketed smallpox
It was that character of the peddler
But they ain't come for trade they came for land
And to find passageways for new settlers
In claiming the new world meant their world was so
Upside down that they needed this new way out
And through rape and pillage of the sanctity
Of this new land would be their escape route
The secular colonists of the Jamestown Settlements
Was London money looking for profits
Then there's the religious group better known as pilgrims
Who made up the other main section of colonists
Though more than a half passed away before the first Winter's passed
In two more the numbers grew like swells
Disease and starvation these self claimed
More civilized beings couldn't feed themselves
Till the Aboriginal people of the land
Taught said man to plant, to seed and thrive
Indentured servants seeking refuge from their homeland
Gave seven or more years of their lives
Till history leads us to believe 1619 is
When Africans sold into slavery first happened
When in 1564 Queen Elizabeth
Funded John Hawkins second quest for African captives
This Manifest Destiny was a planned siege

One only expects growth from planted seeds population was inevitable
Moving into Indian Territory ain't just happen
It was exactly what they set out to do
Like when they set sail for a region
Now known as Australia landing in Tasmania by mistake
With a genocide of force of privateering
Every Tasmanian was erased
Time knows best but let me just speak on this
Dawes Rolls BS I mean y'all see what happened
You can life or death sentence in these courts today
For armed robbery, murder, rape and kidnapping
Slaps to the wrist for those who helped establish this
System Of Money, Power, Respect combativeness
Here you won't find freedom, just captives
Blind trying to claim success amongst the savages
See when Dawes Rolls list writ into law
They basically chose who it was for
Those more rebellious of Indian who may have had success
In battle are those names who won't be on the list
More their bull is these savages so drenched in hatred
Even before they give it back they would try to take it
So under the table was a monkey wrench and
Five bills was all it took to get you documenting
Generations to come this will be beneficent
And here we just peeking in said five dollar Indians

*32

## *15. Manipulated Entertainment*

Election campaigns are manipulated entertainment for the politician in you
Why do you think they are televised
It's to help keep compromising thoughts in our minds
That there's even a choice of who we want to make our decisions for us
Why do you not think it is rigged
Their selections aren't even close to who you would pick
So what do you think it is
Why is it we can't find a politician amongst the people that we can truly back and believe
Why, because we've been programmed to deceive and be deceived
And we deem it necessary to achieve our goals
Preying with prayers
And we expect better conditions
We shouted change and they gave us presidential coins
Meanwhile more black lives have been snatched in the law enforced hand
The overseer's revenge
Since we walking backwards in the time continuum
We gone need our Malcolm X back
Our Martin Luther King
We need a Huey P Newton and Bobby Seale to rise from us
Marcus Garvey, Nelson Mandela, Robert Smalls
We need a Nat Turner amongst us
Sisters we need a Harriet Tubman today
No more thot pics and bad bitch antics displayed
We need our back bones back
Without you, we lack fight
Without fight, we lack change
Without change, we lack free
Mentally, physically
Of their control entirely
Secret society concerned
When the concerns society's secrets
We the whipped been trained
To just lay and take the beatings
Watch and record
Rewind, play and repeat
The broken home pride
Arranged marriage to the streets
All while justice ain't much more than a black man's name
To thee equality that is inlaid yet unclaimed

The scales of balance lean towards the heavier indifference
Concealed in fine print, patent and linguistics
Whose statistics show behavioral studies but truthfully
We just too damn bamboozled in today's buffoonery

*90

## *16. Game or Gamers*

Are we game or gamers
Gridlocked in the mindset
Of today's technology
Wired by the wiring
We are detached from the realisms
Of connecting with each other
We have become disconnected
The tripped on plug
Snatched from the wall of interaction
Locked in the cell
of our phones
pads and tablets
Machinery rendered
We USB synced
In mind and through ear
It appears we
mirror imaging the wickeds
Become the programming
Less than estranged
to scrummaging the grounds
of raped lands
In search of remnants
of sacrilege
Lost tribe descendants
We are lifelines depleting
One hit away from game over
One false flag away from surrender
One computer chip away
from third eye dilation
Charging towards the ring up
Like twelve items or less
We play surge protect of
What in stores self checkout
Oblivious to the blanketed
Chemtrail high of us
We are swung moods in mid-afternoons
False freedom after work shifts
Laborers for their dreams
Bonded by repetition
Till we declare mutiny on hardships
We will board and walk their planks

Old pirate still they rob I
We the target for their Walmart
The martial law marketing
Underestimating the power
Of technological warfare
Mini housed in the squares
of their energy monopolies
Products of their experiments
and projects environmentally
We are one easy going people
one chokehold away from lifeless
one patrol car ride away from stumped bloodlines
one mass shooting away from mausoleum
Train stabled for FEMA
Qualified human cattle
Destined for concentration camps
It's the wave of tomorrow
We consumers of their harvest
Consuming for their Harvest
Till they organ pluck us
We breed the harvested
Survival of the fit
Of the top of the food chain
I'll ask it again
Are we game or gamers

*55

## *17. Provision*

I design lines that redefine rhymes in broken continuum
Capture minds at the door when you visit them
I take the floor like trap doors emitting them
They should case my energy like battery lithium
Feeble cerebrals always seem to get lost in my topics
Though I contact lenses of third blind optics
Atomic plutonium weight don't compare how I drop it
Though I'm shooting for the sun, moon and stars in my cockpit
Logically I ain't screaming I'm iller than nobody
I just cultivate food 'n plant like broccoli
Eat the healthy portions everything else is garnish
I'm not out the neuse using rope to harness
Fast living in the city used to rock jean farmers
Levitated to the south, green thumb...farmers
No disrespect because the first culture is agriculture
Drowned in the footprints left by those who never had a culture
It's a process with progress I quit cigs for the third time
Know exactly what you're thinking should have got it the first time
Excuse is like one running from an unpaid debt
But to move forward sometimes you got to retrace steps
Tempered comfort may succumb to those who do in fact
Try to put their feet back into covered tracks
When it's clear to view that you no longer fit that shoe
Stunted growth can be mental as well as physical
We should all size ourselves we're systematically kept
Those who exclude themselves simply have overslept
In-depth a wealth dreamt was a design to fall
As an individual...in divide you all
Crawl before you walk youth always running to finish lines
Guess statistically that's why we're leaving before our time
See popularity pentacles but peaks are limiting
We've suffered enough self-inflicted prohibiting
From flossing on each other egotistic exhibiting
To killing one another over senseless bickering
Guess Willie's successful, remember when Willie meant you was biggest
We tablespoon fed these outlandish gimmicks
Manipulated Science, Biology and Physics
It's imposed on a slave to praise a false image
Nothing new under the Sun, replicated depictions
Inside these masculine frames, effeminate decisions
Within these sizable garrisons, weak munitions

Been hustled to hustle, tied to a hustlers ambition
See the sight, the vision, incites provision
Illuminate the room like a human filament
Still walking dead in shadowed ignorance
I'll connect bones to bones like the valley's ligaments
I'm from where if you didn't know you learned how
Been where they're in fear of herders after their cow
Once you figure out the fight is futile
The plan to divide and conquer can no longer stand
Don't consider me a showman I don't put on acts
If you enjoy what I spit it's cause you get the facts
Fact is the Matrix got us makeshift in the mental structure
Trying to be better instead of bettering each other
It's war and swords swung no better than guns shot
When within the lands fruit is all we really got
Most get drawn to the sweetness of these poisoned crops
They're actually just feeding off of sick livestock

*22

## *18. Pray Me A Slave*

Be it yesterday's whip
I remain scarred
Those lashes whelped
To remind of when
Recurring imagery is
In kidnap and beating
The mind endures
Daily in today's society
Guess we still enchained
With shackles less tasteful than value
While in volume it's follow the feed
The stream some seem
To drink from guides
The will of those
Next in line
To prison and grave leads
See we Black Friday shopping
Tax refunding ourselves
To a slavery
In support of these things
The schemes against consciousness
We holiday blind
Knowing they ain't
Date Jesus right
So why would they
Date King
Thus we gathering
Record numbers in sales
For groceries and gifts
Is nothing for family
We get these cards
Discounts for information
Further aiding the study
Of where we shop...what we eat
System's a group of things
All working together
To attain the same goal
Therefore control is order
Pile emotion and ego
On top of one another
Improper food, water

And personal space for aura
Self-preservation is human nature
And culturally blind people
Under savage persuasion
Will eat their own kind
Erase the treatment and the labor
From the backs of time
The Lonely at the Top
Never truly reveal the climb
For these crimes against humanity
May none go punished
In fact may you judge
Any whose shadow comes
In resemblance of you
Or your unjust actions
Constitutionally
The black man is only a fraction
So pray me a slave
That I be chained to build your empire
That I be kept unto you
As unclaimed property
That I bring you my ideas
Which you'd fund with ownership
See without you backing me
I mean frontin me, I'm nothing
Pray me a slave that I hate other slaves
So free or caged they will attract my rage
Sex, complexion or age
No matter the weight
Will be a height highest
To my disapproval
Pray Me a slave
A slave of trade
In exchange I'll label for you
I'll Harbor this knowledge
If ever a mustard seed
Of knowledge gained from you
Pray Me a slave
That I noosed neck hang
On your word for your word
Be stronger than oak
The branch that barks
Holding the limbs

Of young black men
To this day, Pray Me a slave
To the God taught to slaves
To the processed foods
And insecticide sprays
To the propaganda
That the news displays
To the over the counter drugs
And street drugs the same
A slave, to the currency exchange
To the miseducation
Incarcerating the brain
To the cattle housing
Of the prison game
To the fear, anger and pain
For the lives you've slain...pray
Pray me a slave
Be it just that
In your prayers
I'll be
A slave

*8

## *19. Mindfood (Food For Thought) Pt. 2*

Many  times I clutch my soul feeling hollow
Sipping on wines as if there's no tomorrow
Follow no leader for I know not where they're leading
Nor do I eat from everyone some know not what they're feeding
The uncivilized is simply trapped in their self
How can one control violence when all crave wealth
In padlocked plans to understand us ebonics was a tool
Won't truth us of our origin yet street slang in school
Who's fooling who we go back past slavery
To die like a thug is foolishness not bravery
It's plain to see that we are not equally accounted for
As in that independency we share each seven four
I am not a dog nor is my sister a bitch
I want to reestablish the respect lost in the bridge
To condemn us to the ghetto and label us nuisance
Is simply raping our freedoms with little to no lubrance
I see pass cover for ingredients is deeper
Though life is priceless, death is no cheaper
The war is not amongst us there's bigger fish to fry
Been killing ourselves, when we hate to see mom's cry

## *20. Nameless Bullets*

It's a new year
Don't go killing nights air
With nameless bullets
If you ain't ready to take a bullet
Every 38 hours the past few hundred hours
Several times on the hour
With black youth in the footage
Authorities over majority
Authorized or unauthorized
Violate lives of Youth
Or are we hallucinating
Here where lives are chained to laws
Laws are chained to the lives
The state rules to execute
Is a true understatement
Are we misunderstood or targeted
Any who misunderstand what target is
A person object or place
Attempted to aim at
I see us I see them
Aiming where we at
Awaiting an aim back
Awaken and aim back
Keep shooting up the sky
There'll be nothing to aim back
It's a new year
Don't go killing night's air with nameless bullets
If you ain't ready to take a bullet
What goes up must come down
Damage and distance of travel
Depend on force of weapon
Caliber and path of the bullet
These segments of firing
That signified success
The year brought to us
Is a false sense of accomplishment
Instead of the sky
We need to target the issues
Till the injustices endured
Reach abolishment
Spare night's sky that pain

That rain of ammunition
That raucous outroar
That rein over children
Enslaving, they slay
And make prey of our children
See we own one of them
Before our own pot to piss in
It's a new year
Don't go killing nights air
With nameless bullets
If you ain't ready to take a bullet
Openly shooting us down
While we stand with phone cameras
Reconstructing social networks
With black youth in the footage
Sedated crowds, trials televised
Judiciary landslides
No real consequences
For the deaths of black lives
You all know the verdicts
But where common sense resides
Other than self-defense
Homicide is homicide
Under rugs we find
Cadavers of hate crimes
Many have been murdered
While the camera played blind
It’s peri mental times
Giving sight to blind eyes
Just fighting to survive
Where human organs advertised
Is ill….
But it's a new year
Don't go killing night’s air
With nameless bullets
If you ain't ready to take a bullet

*74

## *21. Chemtrails*

We were caught with our heads in the clouds.
Clouds of truck and train smoke matched in blocks of chain smokers.
Trash cans on fire.
Brush fire forests layering the unawaring blue appearance of the sky.
Made it easy to conceive how pollution wounded the ozone.
Devastating to our reality.
That is what they told us.
What they scientifically theorized.
Vicarious existence.
Man's facetious behavior resulted in global warming.
Our heads in the clouds.
Those heavy words caught in the wind change.
Doomsday film melting in the thaw of the polar caps.
He would counterattack.
Once again man has declared war.
Weaponized chemical warfare
welcome the delivery of precursor sulfide gases.
Hydrogen sulfide, sulfur dioxide and sulfuric acid.
Into the atmosphere.
Our natural breathing air.
As if nature was in need of a cure.
it was a means to an end of all that would be natural.
Oxygen being detrimental to all living things agricultural to mammal.
they had to know there'd be side effects
Like every other medication given by man.
Is this why I find myself ducking aircrafts across the sky.
Fear of waking in congestion.
Dry dripping nasal cavities.
Your "raid spray" side effects
acting as a pollen allergy.
I can't breathe resisting the chokehold
of jet streaming skyfall.
Your net like cloud patterns of
stratospheric sulphate aerosols.
Declared war against the sun
using reflective nano materials.
Sounds like G. I. Joe covert op'ed some real cobra shit.
Snake on belly scaling the temple of the naive.
No longer chasing the storm.
Now you openly cause them.

Tell us they did not form Katrina
Maria nor Irma.
Yet the design is to in fact get water to dry places.
All while we can't get clean water in Flint Michigan.
Got you, looking to Wakanda like Africa denied you.
There are no bigger secrets than here on the very land you was birthed to.
The rescue/takeover team.
We give a lot of ourselves don't we.
I mean we give and give to be an under heavy deficit country.
Must be the blocking out the sun,
the blocking out the light.
The smog of exterminates
blocking out all means for me
to see,
to breathe,
cohesion.
While separated from the energy of the cosmos.
Quit smothering me under reflective artificial clouds.
Repelling at my chi in attempt to dim my aura.
My melanation cries for absorbing the Sun's rays.
It's skin kiss is an aid agent to my performance.
Light is truth and all that lives reaches for it
Be wise you stop trying to force man into dark spaces.
Harnessing your energy into hatred of a black whole.
When all of darkness is what comes from the blocking out of light.
Is this the reasoning for your blanketing the sky.
Blanketing the night.
To disguise Star Wars.
Keep the tamed man grounded.
Had to know there'd be side effects.
Fooling with nature this way.
Chemical bombing the essence of the ancestors among us.
Directing all that is into an extinction level event.
Disrupting the natural way of everything living.
Maybe one day we will get our heads out of the clouds.

*86

www.ingramcontent.com/pod-product-compliance
Ingram Content Group UK Ltd.
Pitfield, Milton Keynes, MK11 3LW, UK
UKHW041905190726
13854UKWH00003B/1091

9 781387 614196